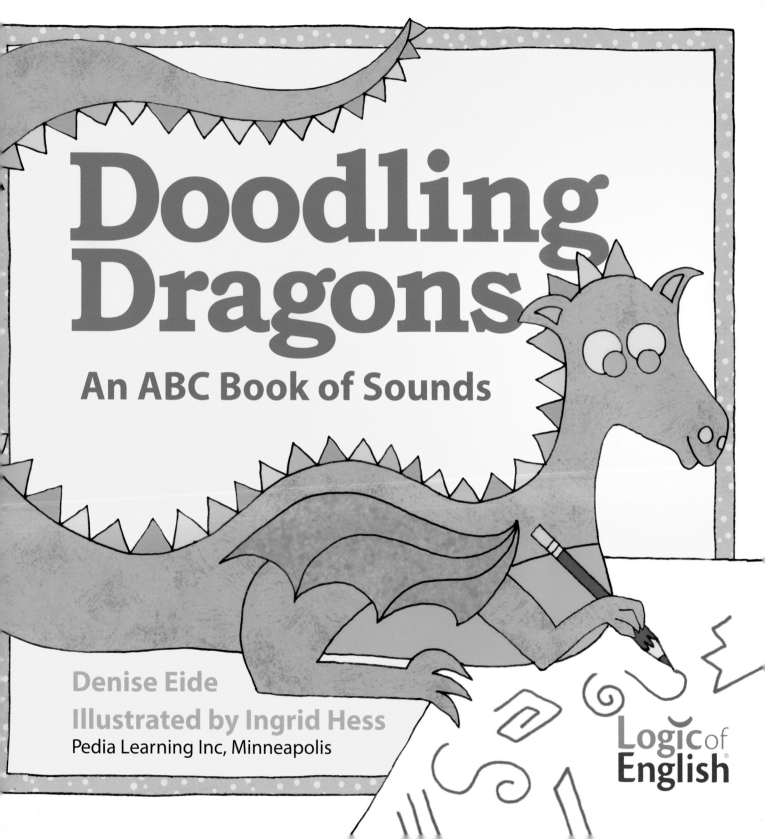

Doodling Dragons

An ABC Book of Sounds

Denise Eide

Illustrated by Ingrid Hess

Pedia Learning Inc, Minneapolis

Logic of English

Doodling Dragons: An ABC Book of Sounds

Copyright © 2013 Logic of English, Inc

Logic of English, Inc
4871 19th Street NW, Suite 110
Rochester, MN 55901
United States of America

First Edition
Fourth Printing

Printed in the United States of America

ISBN 978-1-936706-22-8

10 9 8 7 6 5 4

Tips for Enjoying *Doodling Dragons*

How to help children develop an awareness that letters represent sounds.

• Read the sound(s) made by each phonogram; emphasize the sounds, not the letter names.

• Point to the phonogram as you say the sound(s).

• Ask the child to repeat the sound when you point to the phonogram.

• Ask the child to find the phonogram within the words on the page.

• Ask the child to think of other words that include the sound.*

> * If the child lists words that use a different spelling for the sound, that is fine. The goal is to develop awareness of sounds; precise spellings will come later.

Notes to Parents:

• A phonogram is a picture of a sound. All words in English are written with a combination of phonograms. There are 74 basic phonograms.

• This book introduces the A-Z phonograms; to read fluently students will need to learn an additional 48 multi-letter phonograms.

• Qu is a multi-letter phonogram in English which says /kw/. Q always needs a U. U is not a vowel here.

Encourage your child's awareness of sounds!

A

/ă-ā-ä/

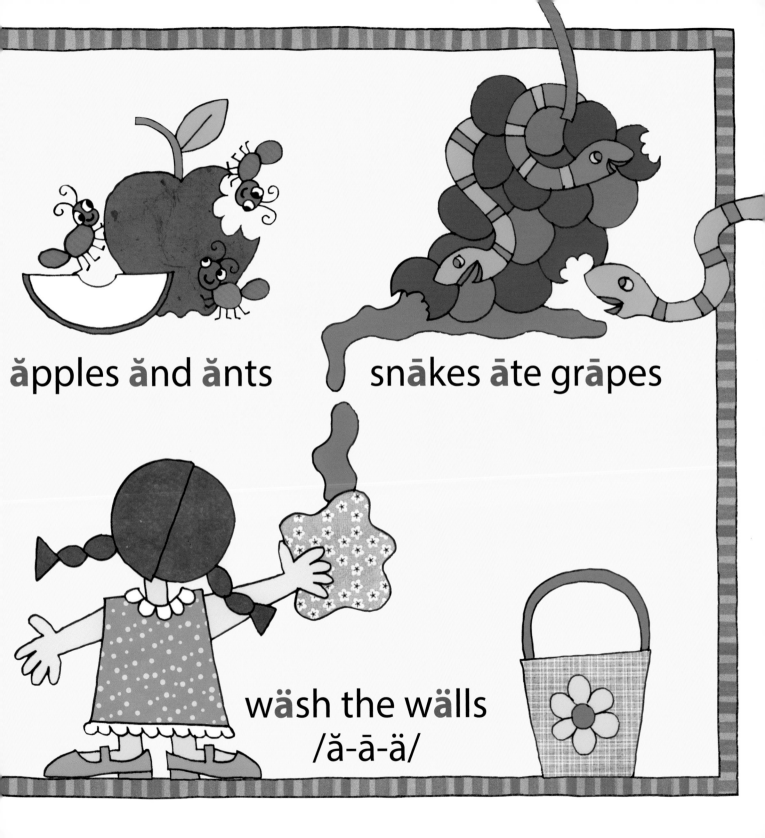

ăpples ănd ănts   snākes āte grāpes

wäsh the wälls
/ă-ā-ä/

B

b

/b/

barking **b**eagle
buttered **b**read
blowing **b**ub**b**les
baby's **b**ed

C c

/k-s/

cards, di**c**e

crackers, ri**c**e

circus **c**lown

casting **c**rowns

D

d

/d/

doo**d**ling **d**ragons
dollars, **d**imes
darling **d**imples
dad**d**y **d**ines

E

/ĕ-ē/

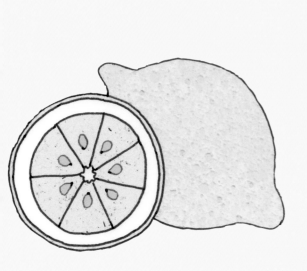

yĕllow lĕmons

ĕmerald shĕlves

ēmus ēmailing

ēvil ĕlves

F

f

/f/

fluttering **f**airies
fancy **f**an
fighting **f**ires
fisherman

G

g

/g-j/

green **g**iants   **g**org**e**ous **g**ems

golden **g**erbils   **gi**ng**e**rbread men

H

/h/

hugging **h**edge**h**ogs
honeybee
heavy **h**ammer
huge **h**umvee

I i

/ĭ-ī-ē-y/

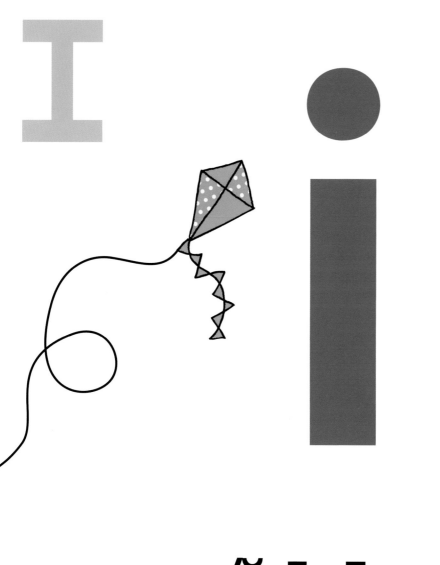

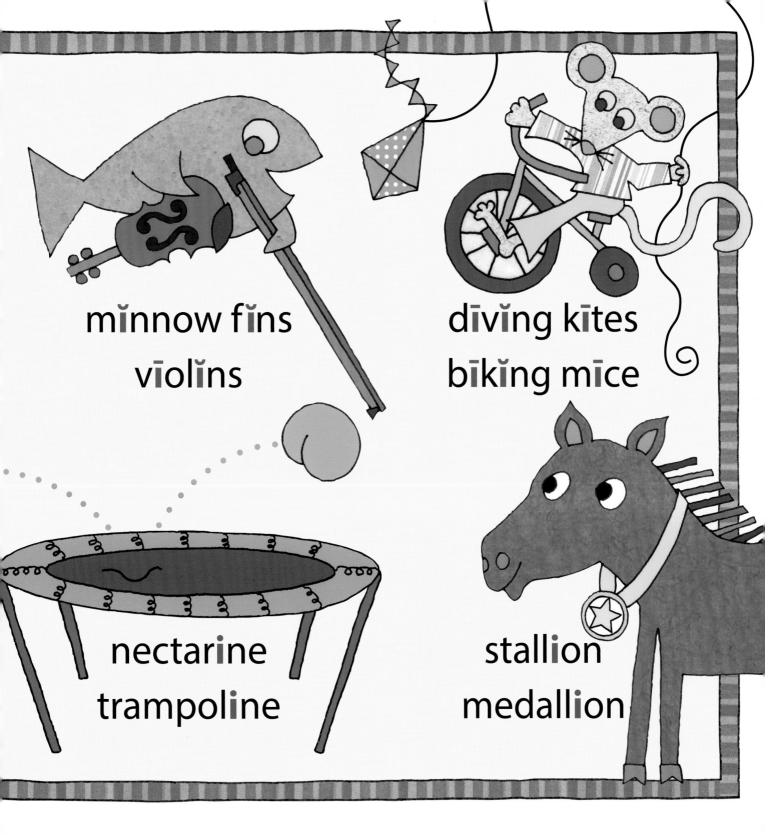

mĭnnow fĭns
vīolĭns

dīvĭng kītes
bīkĭng mīce

nectarine
trampoline

stallion
medallion

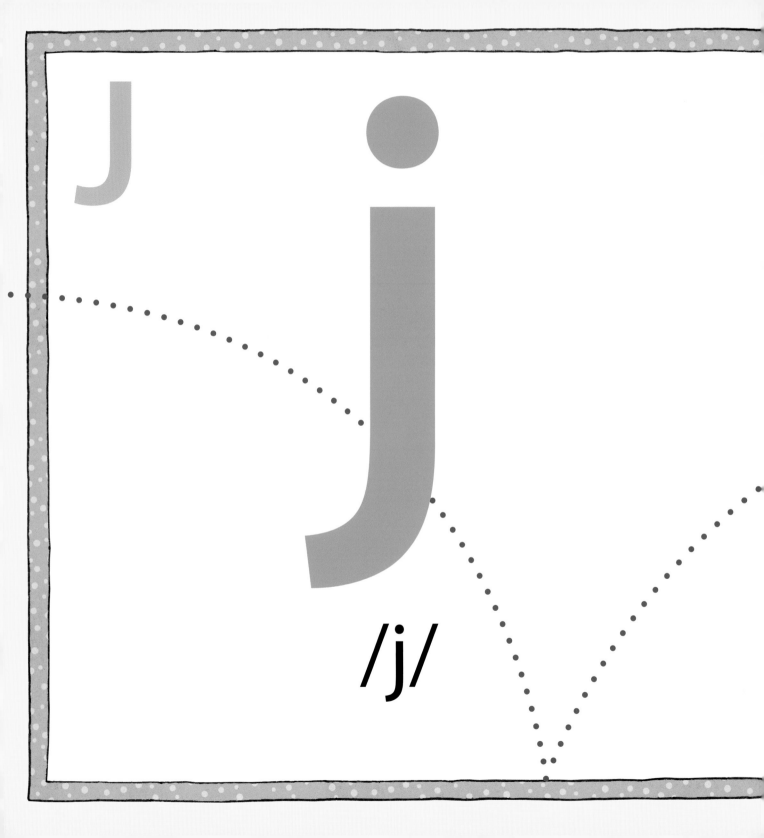

J j

/j/

jittery jellyfish
in a jar
juggling jack
Jump! Jaguar!

K

k

/k/

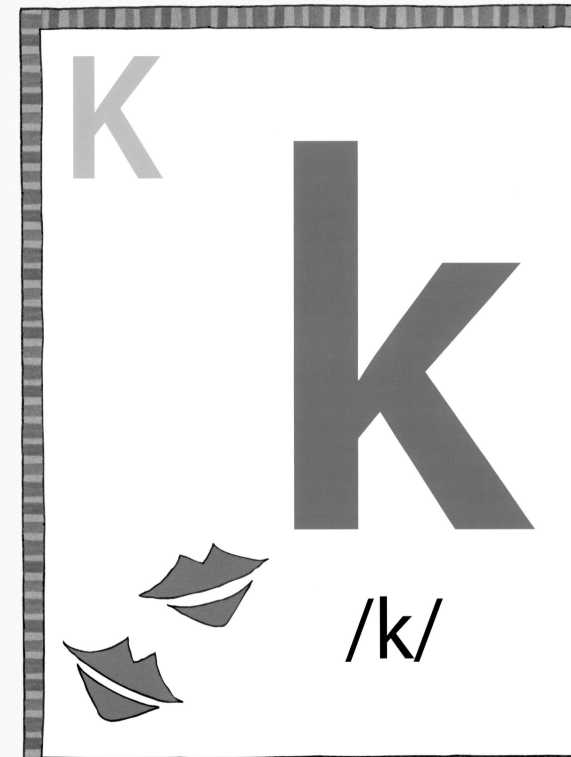

klutzy **k**itten

Katie's **k**ite

koala **k**isses

the **k**ing's bi**k**e

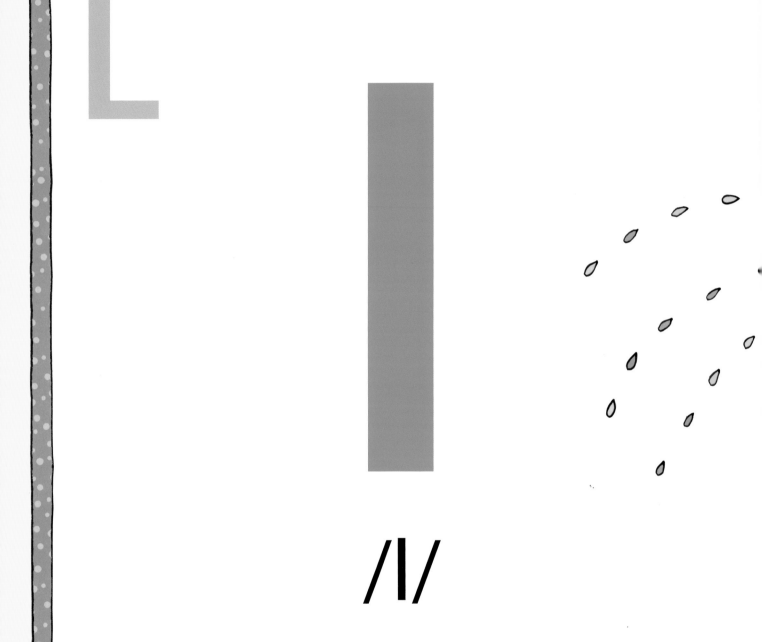

licking lemons
lighting lamps
leaping lemur
locking clamp

M

m

/m/

munching **m**angos

masquerade

milk and **m**uffins

marm**a**lade

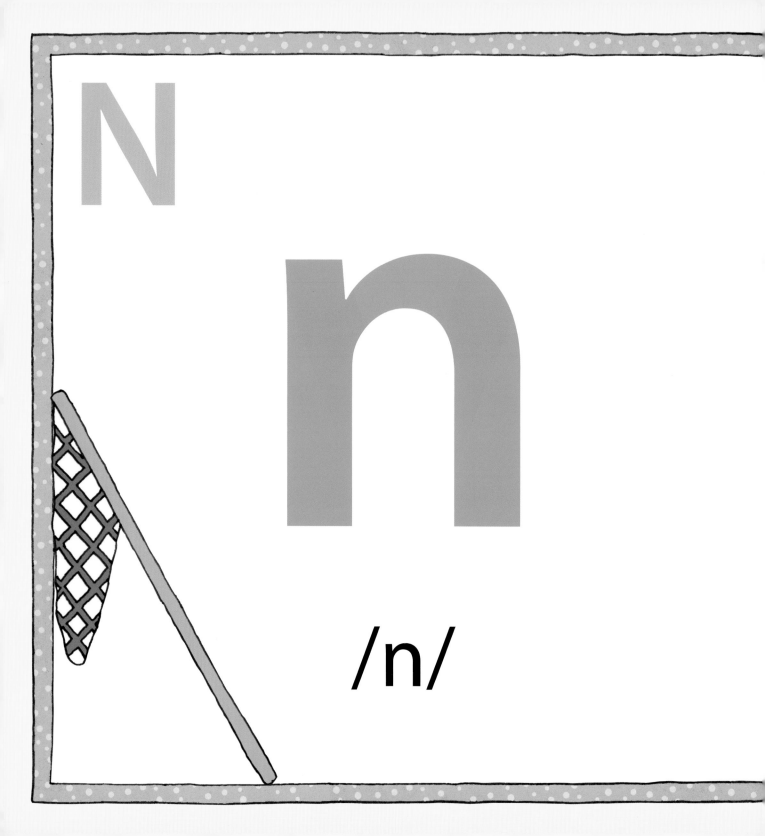

ni**n**etee**n** **n**oodles
nylo**n** **n**et
noisy **n**urses
mario**n**ette

/ŏ-ō-ö/

Stŏp! Hŏp!

Gō ŏn hōme!

Whö can dö it?

Möve it! Pröve it!

P

p

/p/

pink **p**ajamas
pretty **p**lates
pu**pp**y's **p**aws
pur**p**le skates

Quickly, **qu**eens!   Give a **squ**eeze!

Quit that **qu**acking!   **Qu**iet please!

R

r

/r/

reindeer run
rabbits romp
robins trill
gorillas tromp

s

S

/s-z/

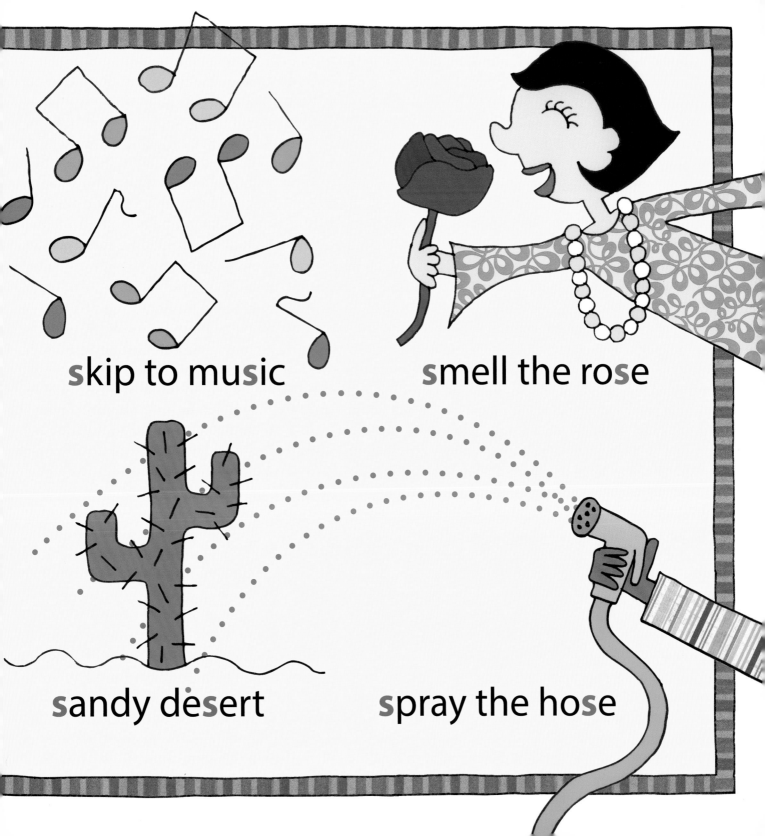

skip to music

smell the rose

sandy desert

spray the hose

T t

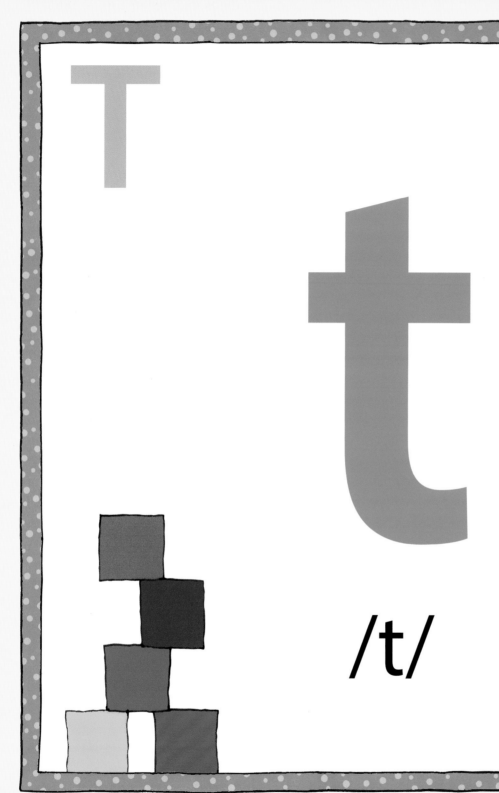

/t/

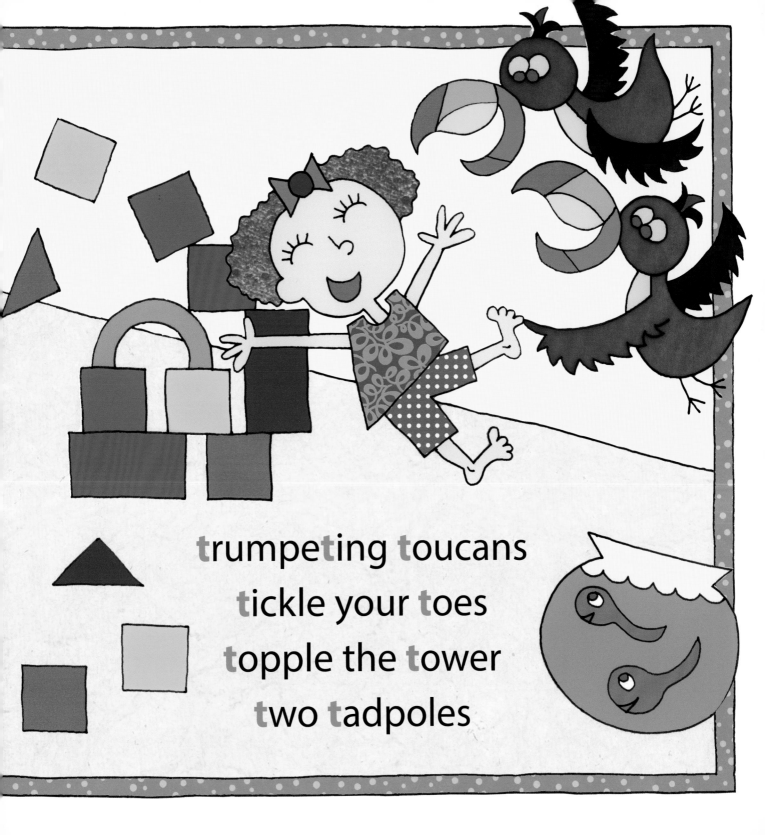

trumpe**t**ing **t**oucans
tickle your **t**oes
topple the **t**ower
two **t**adpoles

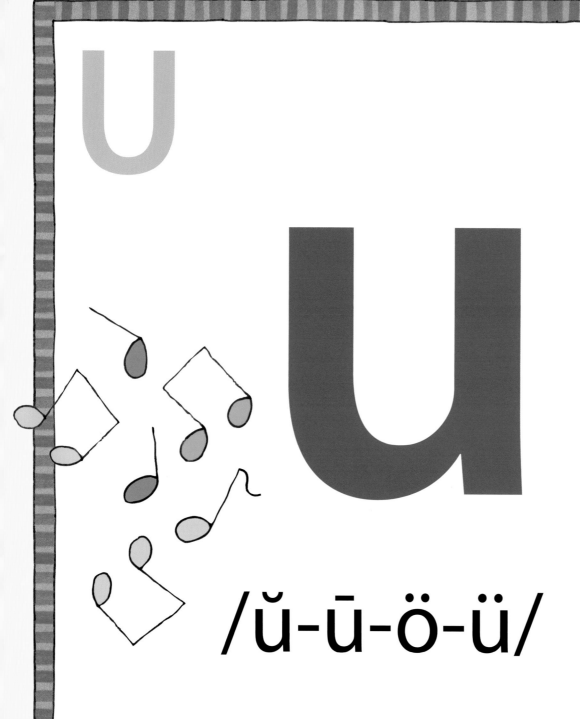

U u

/ŭ-ū-ö-ü/

ŭncle's ŭgly ŭnderwear

būgle mūsic everywhere

tubas tuning parachuting

pŭt the bŭtcher in the pŭdding

V v

/v/

vultures, do**v**es
ho**v**er abo**v**e
mo**v**ing, swer**v**ing
wea**v**ing, cur**v**ing

W

/w/

wishful **w**olves

wearing **w**igs

wispy **w**illows

snapping t**w**igs

wily **w**izards

on a **w**ire

Water! **W**ater!

Wildfire!

x

X

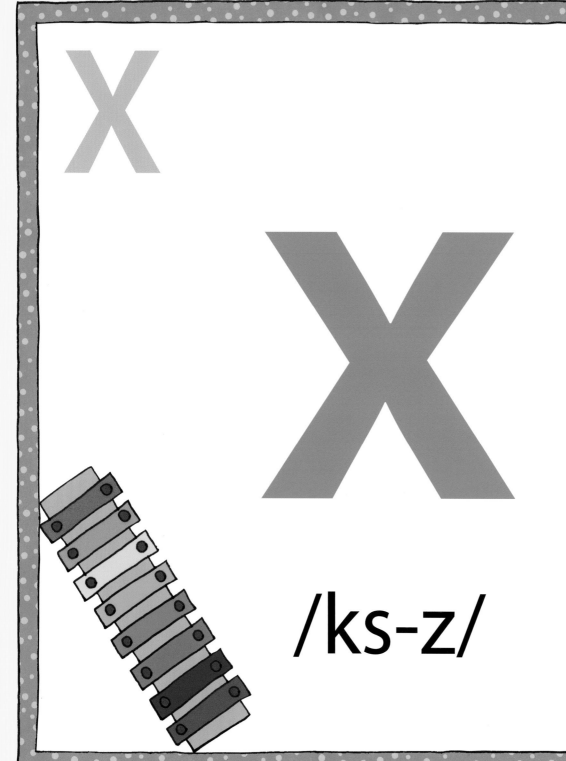

/ks-z/

toolbo**x**es
sa**x**ophone
si**x** wa**x** o**x**en
xylophone

Y

y

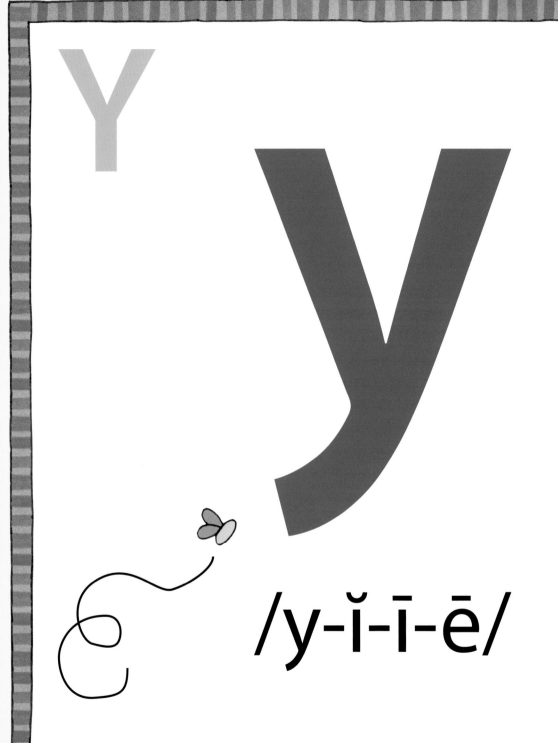

/y-ĭ-ī-ē/

Yodelers **y**elling,
"**Y**ummy **y**ams!"

m**y**stery cr**y**stal
g**y**mnast jams

H**y**enas t**y**ping,
"Good-b**y**e fl**y**!"

"Mudd**y** pupp**y**!"
bab**y** cries.

Z z

/z/

fuzzy buzzard

lizard freezes

winter blizzard

zebra sneezes

Other Products by Logic of English

- **Uncovering the Logic of English: A Common-Sense Approach to Reading, Spelling, and Literacy**

- **Logic of English Foundations Curriculum**
  A Reading, Spelling and Writing Program for Ages 4-7

- **Foundations Readers**
  Levels B, C, and D

- **Logic of English Essentials Curriculum**
  Multi-Level Reading, Spelling, Grammar & Vocabulary

- **The Essentials Reader**

- **Phonogram and Spelling Game Book**

- **Phonogram Game Cards**

- **Phonogram Game Tiles**

- **Phonogram Flash Cards**

- **Spelling Rule Flash Cards**

- **Rhythm of Handwriting Series**

www.LogicOfEnglish.com

Logic of English®